A cup of butterflies & birdsongs

by MAC

illustrated by Carol Auel

Published by
CompCare publications
Minneapolis, Minnesota
A division of Comprehensive Care Corporation

© 1976 by MAC

All rights reserved.
Published in the United States
by CompCare Publications.

Library of Congress Catalog Card
No. 76-55450

Reproduction in whole or part, in
any form, including storage in
memory device or system, is
forbidden without written
permission... except that portions
may be used in broadcast or printed
commentary or review when
attributed fully to authors and
publication by names.

Dedication

You walked through those days
          with me ...
And you held my hand,
As God and my hand wrote
          most of these poems.

God understands
Why I dedicate them to you
          anonymously ...
Although I was tempted to have your name printed
          repeatedly on this page,
          in different directions,

God knows
How slow
Recovery is.

How treasured, symbolical, the
          butterfly ...
And how hard to let go.

Butterflies are not to keep—
First person to read my book—
But as I let go, faith and love take
          me full circle
Into God's larger fellowship.

I'm so grateful we touch.

Help, when you need it . . .

Acceptance/Resentments
Another Acceptance 13
Fruition 55
I Give You 4 Quarters and You Give Me $1 45
Mechanic 39
Pinch Hitter 44
Separation 65
Spring Cleaning 52
Walking with God 90
Why Me? 85

Action/Procrastination
A Valentine for My Child 25
Practicing My Stable Tables 24
Preservation 91
What Length? 23

Faith/Fear
Belief Is Knowledge of the Heart 60
Bridge Building 41
Christmas Without Manger 75
I Learn from the Snowflakes 18
Layover 64
Morning Glory Loom 56
Prodigal Daughter 61
Snowshoes of Faith, The 19
Spiritual Blackout 58

Teach Me to Pray, God 35
Turning It Over 34
Walking Together 40

Forgiving/Judgmental
After the Trees are Chopped Down 27
Brothers and Sisters 29
80 Miles of Bad Road 89
Organic Growth 26
Downtown Christmas 76

Gratitude/Negative Thinking
Birth Announcement 37
Candle Lighting 74
Giving Thanks 73
Mechanic 39
Miracle of the Pussy Willows, The 50
Morning Song 12
Mother's Day Bouquet 57
One Fine Day at a Time 93
Seeing the Rain Through Uplifted Eyes 30
Sobriety is a Sunrise 94
Spring Shower 31

Happiness/Depression
A Cup of Bird Songs and Sunrise 7
Giving Thanks 73
Leaf Raking 68
Leaving My Own Prison 15
Looking Up Today in Your Dictionary 46
Mother's Day 54
Preservation 91
Spiritual Blackout 58
Spring Birth 47
Tears Turn Into Shining 14
Walking My Hardest Length 17

Honesty/Dishonesty
Admitting Myself 53
Coming Ashore 51
First Prayer 8
Ruination, the Foundation 78
Spring Cleaning 52
Turning in the Empties for You 70

Humanism/Perfectionism
  Downtown Christmas **76**
  Happy Road, The **42**
  Quiz for the Living **88**
  Salvation Song for an Ant **69**
  Three Forward, Two Back **48**

Humility/False Pride
  First Prayer **8**
  Into Reality **66**
  Peeling Off My Facial Mask **71**
  Seven Veils of Autumn Fall, The **67**
  Unfolding, the Imperfect Rose **31**
  Why Me? **85**

Order/Confusion
  In an Emergency, Halt! **84**
  Into Reality **66**
  Mechanic **39**
  Momentary Success **72**
  Morning Song **12**
  Spring Birth **47**
  Throwing a Kiss at Myself in the Mirror **10**
  Turning It Over **34**

Patience/Frustration
  A Peony Doesn't Blossom in a Day **32**
  Accepting Blizzards **22**
  Organic Growth **26**
  Pinch Hitter **44**
  Polishing My Soul in the Rough **43**
  Sewing My Patchwork Quilt **11**
  Three Forward, Two Back **48**
  Two Year Old Blues with an Upbeat **80**
  Walking with God **90**

Peace/Anger
  Accepting Blizzards **22**
  I Give You 4 Quarters and You Give Me $1 **45**
  Learning to Accept the Loss **21**
  Separation **65**
  Why Me? **85**

Self-Respect/Guilt Feelings
  Becoming a Hand **87**
  Mother's Day **54**
  Preservation **91**
  Threefold Healing **95**
  Who Am I to Criticize the Master? **38**
  Without Excuse **9**

Self-Esteem/Self-Pity
  Another Acceptance **13**
  Fruition **55**
  Leaving My Own Prison **15**
  Outstretched Hand, The **81**
  Ready or Not, Get Off the Pity Pot **86**
  Tears Turn Into Shining **14**
  Why Me? **85**

Serenity/Insanity
  A Cup of Bird Songs and Sunrise **7**
  Belief is Knowledge of the Heart **60**
  Into Reality **66**
  Outstretched Hand, The **81**
  Practicing My Stable Tables **24**
  Spiritual Blackout **58**
  Spring Birth **47**
  Throwing a Kiss at Myself in the Mirror **10**
  Turning It Over **34**

Sharing/Selfishness
  Becoming a Hand **87**
  Help on the Road **79**
  Madame Butterfly Learning to Do the Twelfth Step **62**
  Outstretched Hand, The **81**
  Quiz for the Living **88**
  Snowbells **92**

Tolerance/Intolerance
  A Peony Doesn't Blossom in a Day **32**
  I Give You 4 Quarters and You Give Me $1 **45**
  Relativity **59**
  Snow Sonnet **83**
  Who Am I to Criticize the Master? **38**

Foreword

I'm an alcoholic and an addict in recovery.

Much of the help with my recovery has come from self-help programs, but I also have received help from social agencies, psychiatric clinics, medical doctors, institutions, jail and the courts. So many of my brothers and sisters on this planet have contributed to my recovery that I could never estimate the number. How many stars are there in the sky?

Today I am dry and clean and growing in sobriety. I can't tell you how grateful I am for the fact that my heart still beats.

My "bottom" before seeking help was very low. Several times I was hospitalized and sent to a mental institution before being sent to an alcoholic unit at a state hospital. I was arrested three times and served a 15-day jail sentence. For ten years I underwent psychiatric therapy, bordering (a doctor once told me) on suicide or lifetime institutionalization.

I did not know who I was, or, at that time in my life, which one of me I was. God has slowly and gradually restored me.

These are the poems given to me by God and people. They are the words I heard, learned, felt, breathed and received. I've only set them into rhythm, rhyme, symbol, metaphor like a technician. I have prayed before, after, and through them, asking constantly for God's help with them.

I know who I am today. I'm you, or the person sitting next to you. I'm an alcoholic and addict in recovery, dry and clean today, growing in sobriety.

A cup of bird songs and sunrise

The birds wake up the morning
With songs of sunrise, pouring
Their laughter through the air,
Gilding the limbs everywhere
Around them with that burnished
Joy, that awakening from a furnace,
That makes the songs of those birds,
Like hands reaching out, understood.

First prayer

I've been conning myself.
I'm phony as hell,
But I never needed You
As I do now.

I want to stop drinking
More than I want to.
I'm a drunk! Dear God!
Help me do what I can't do.

Alone, so terribly alone.
My whole life's been a bender.
Here, in a blizzard, shivering,
All of these pieces surrender.

Without excuse

My soul's porch was
A garden of cement,
Cracked like a slum.
Through that broken lament
Of sidewalk that knew
Of tropical gardens,
A cornflower grew.
It broke its way
From decadent soil,
Rolling leaves above elbows,
Ready for the toil
Of growing there
Underfoot, to survive
Hell and its henchmen,
Determined to live.

Throwing a kiss at myself in the mirror

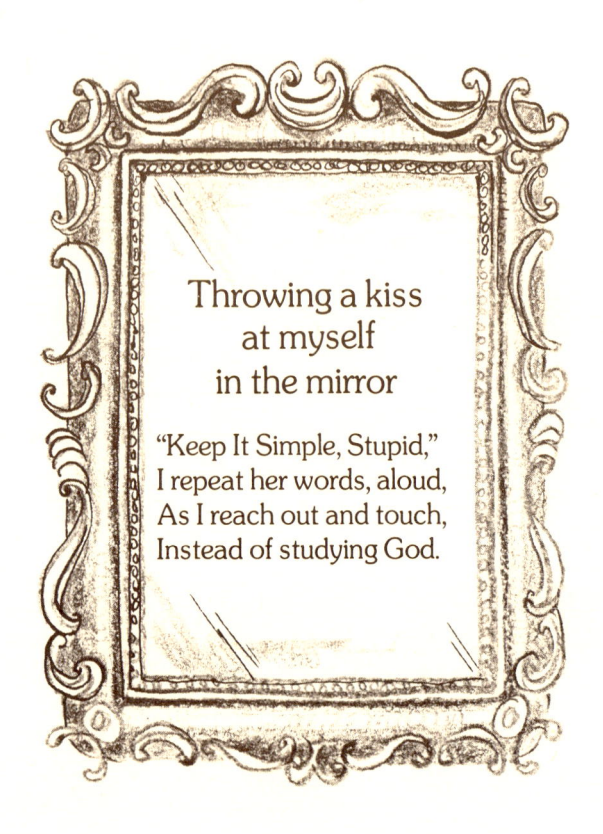

"Keep It Simple, Stupid,"
I repeat her words, aloud,
As I reach out and touch,
Instead of studying God.

Sewing my
patchwork quilt

I stitch into place
A patch made of denim,
For this is today's patch
I have been given.

I don't even question
Your quilt's design,
But just add a patch
One day at a time.

Morning song

"Good God! It's morning!"
She used to say,
Waking to her hangover's
Winced look at the day.

Now that she's sober
She's turned it around.
"Good Morning, God!"
Is her awakened song.

Another acceptance

I don't like being an epileptic.
I'd rather not be one.
But this is the body
I have been given.

Shall I use illness
As an excuse
To return to my pills
Or drink poisonous booze,

Adding to my problems
A hundred fold?
If I do, I'm apt to die
Or go nutty instead of growing old.

Gratefully, I'm treatable
One day at a time.
Wondrously I'm alive,
With a sound mind.

Tears turn into shining

I used to cry with Titihoya
Watering all my discords.
My life turned into rebel vines
Of unmanageable orchids.

Today I shine with dawning's
Brilliant gratitudes,
As You bless with morning satin
My own soul's attitude.

Leaving my own prison

I do not need this pity.
I leave it in the dark,
Like an empty locust shell
Clinging to the bark.

Walking my hardest length

The three of them are standing there,
I do not think they understand this prayer
I must walk alone, but I am aware
Of theirs,
Just as difficult. Like a stairs,
These steps ascend difficult airs
To a living place where,
If we dare,
We shall no longer have to strive
Merely to stay alive.
My oldest son hugs me, and in his face
Is a proud peace.
My daughter cries of this separation
In her father's arms.
And bright as sunshine, wishing me well,
Waves the youngest miracle girl.
I smile, laughing, clenching the cry
In my throat, hugging the baby like a lullaby.

I learn from the snowflakes

Snowflakes as delicate as bird's wings
Float in the rhythm that the wind sings,
Easily doing what comes naturally,
And doing it satisfactorily
In Your large blue hand
Of my own understanding.

The snowshoes of faith

When I am lost in a spiritual blizzard,
And the drifts seem to cover my feet,
With Your help I slowly move forward.
Faith makes wide snowshoes for traveling
Through buried streets.

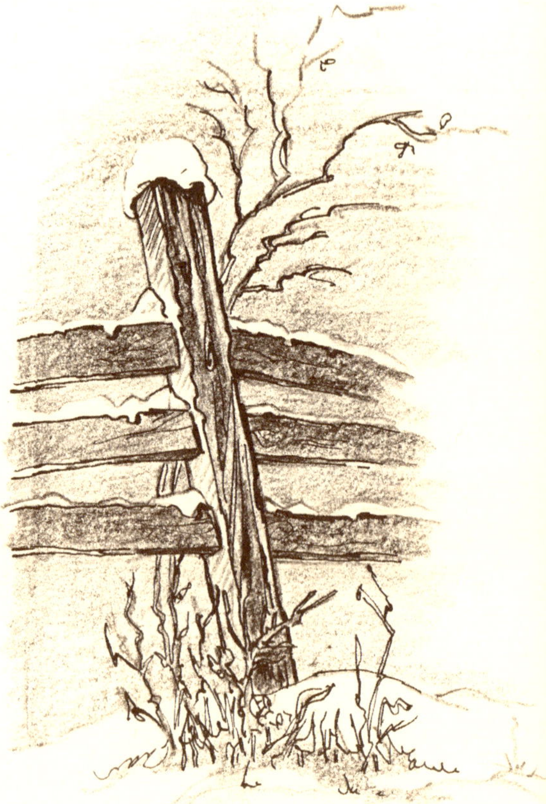

Learning to accept the loss

It is winter
And the hospital lawn
Spreads out like a nurse's
Uniform;
The hospital is gone,
Like a lost doctor, like a lost
Friend.
Their words, in this
Recovered sky blue season,
Eternally return, flake upon flake,
Within.

Accepting blizzards

Today's a blizzard.
Now, don't get me wrong.
There's no way I want back
That old life with its frozen song,
But today's a blizzard.
Give me Your hand,
And help me walk through it,
Accepting that all life can't be rose grand.

What length?

Did I leave my Big Book on the shelf
Because my only light,
Flames from the burning hearth,
Might hurt my sight?

Did I want to read it so badly
I walked mile after mile to borrow
A copy today, or did I
Decide to wait for tomorrow?

Practicing my stable tables

I practice patience
Like mathematical tables.
God knows I have enough facts,
But need practice, practice, practice, to become more stable.

A valentine for my child

I cook her eggs for breakfast,
And iron her a shirt
To match the handstitched gingham
Of her granny skirt.
With You, I keep me sober
For another day,
And bake some oatmeal cookies.
She hurts a child in play.
I call her in from out of doors,
And send her to her room,
Amid protesting "I hate you!" 's,
Part of a mother's tunes.
At end of day I hand her
My only valentine,
Explaining that the action
Far excels the rhyme.

Organic growth

You didn't make prefabricated mountains,
Nor instant rivers with assembly line rocks.
Likewise, You didn't throw me into a machine
And crank me out, perfectly working the steps.
I, with Your help, had to crawl in order to walk.

After
the trees
are chopped down

I clear away my mistakes,
Like cherry trees, each day
As best I can.
"I'm sorry," I say,
Planting new trees.
I'm only a human
Who can't possibly
Do it perfectly,
But can do it. And
I find
It brings peace of mind.

Brothers and sisters

I remember autumn's naked trees,
Arching in an agonous breeze,
As they tried with their souls to blossom with leaves.
Through that long winter, I saw in each face,
   Fear, faith, and struggle, each in its place,
      And learned how to pray, "Saved by the grace..."
         Some do not make it. They fall on the stairs,
            Burning in flames. I pray with them there,
               Glad in our souls of the recovery I wear.

Seeing the rain through uplifted eyes

Through your eyes, uplifted,
Like a gift,
You show me rain,
Re-explained.
The drops of rain
Come down,
Soft hymns,
Releasing the pressure within.

Spring shower

At busy day's intersection,
I see a sign to cross,
And in my soul, on Oxford street,
Magnolia blossoms toss.

The petals fall, like blessings.
I know they come from You,
As, gratitude on gratitude,
Those petals fill my soul.

A peony doesn't blossom in a day

The buds on the stem
Unfold slowly, one after one,
Explaining the rhythm
Of nature's pendulum.

Unfolding, the imperfect rose

Slowly, it starts to unfold,
Thorns, leaves, petals and rust,
It sees within its own blossom.
It begins to trust.

Turning it over

My life, I am turning it over,
Giving it back to You,
For You kept me alive when
   my soul was dead,
And my mind was black and blue.

Like seeds, I'm receiving Your will.
Slowly they grow into
Bright lilies that nourish my soul,
And lead me closer to You.

Teach me to pray, God...

Teach me to pray, God,
To reach out, like dark sod,
Unafraid of the seed of Your word.

Teach me to pray, Father,
To You, no other,
Whatever the weather,

Stormy, or fair,
Help me wear prayer.

Birth announcement

I don't remember ever
Hurting worse
Than when I was in labor,
Giving birth;
And the last time, five
Months dry,
Was worse than any
Of the other three.
I went through a
Terrible setback,
Physically, spiritually
And emotionally,
Feeding the little guy
Around the clock,
And tied down to one
More responsibility.
I don't plan to have
Anymore.
Many girls, after a birth,
Return to the bar.

But this child that I'm
raising, clearly
Able to see, the eyes change
Color, nearly
Able to speak in his
Foreign tongue,
Though he's heavy at times,
He's my son!

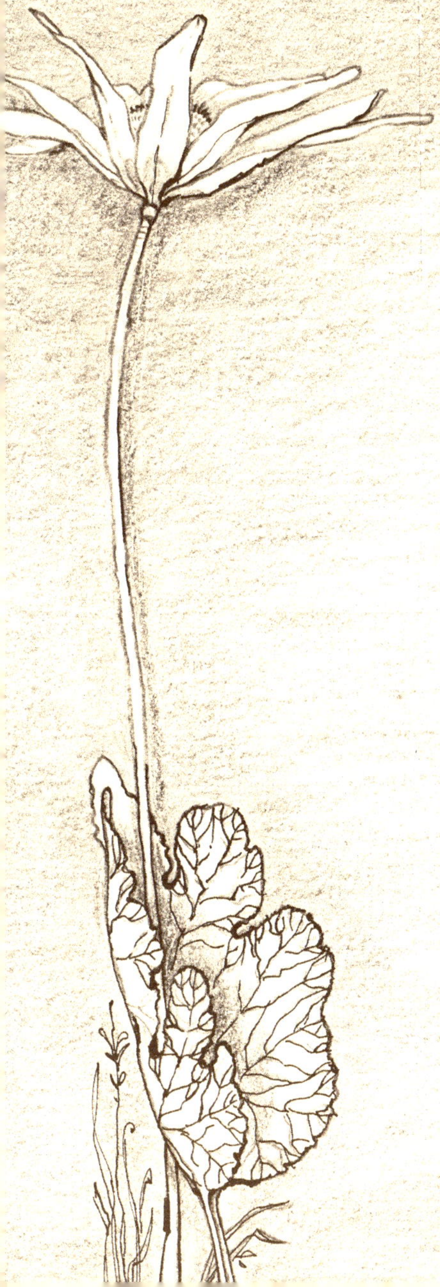

Who am I to criticize the Master?

When my thoughts
Are too defunct,
And I'm totalling myself again,
I try to remember
You don't make junk,
And I'm part of Your Master Plan.

Mechanic

I take it apart, and turn it over,
For when it is broken down
And reorganized, I discover
The wonder of God's mind.

Walking together

Spirits meet,
However far
Apart
The streets.

Bridge building

I'm building a bridge across a stream,
Working, sweating, and often stopping
               To sit on the bank with You.

The bridge is sturdy as it leaves my hand,
And I know that my slowness You understand
               As I offer each plank to You.

For I have hurried to build before,
And plummeted the depths of an unsound floor.
               I sank when I let go of You.

A slow bridge built by hands that are weak
Enough to reach out to You for strength,
Might take a lifetime, as I gradually seek
To span the stream from bank to bank,
My labor my gift of humble thanks
                For these planks that bring me toward You.

The happy road

The walk through flames to finally
Get here
(Not the words that monks have painted
With embellishment and care),

The journey through the darkened
valley
Only You and I have traveled;
Up each mountain, through each gulley,

Unfold my steps, faltering,
But still
Rising from each fall, You help me
Turn into Your chosen tool.

Polishing my soul in the rough

Your will is like a cloth
I use upon my soul
To rub away my defects
And, inward, glow.
Sometimes I hesitate
In moving toward Your Light.
Adversity adds weight,
And helps remove the blight.

Pinch hitter

Exams were coming up.
Anxiety set in.
I studied as best I could
For my mark of recognition.

Finally I surrendered,
Not knowing what to do.
Dean's list You earned for me,
And I earned for You.

I give you 4 quarters
          and
          you give me $1

> I cannot change a cardinal
> Into a cherry.
> I cannot change a marigold
> Into a canary.
> I cannot make a sidewalk,
> Like a river, flow.
> I can only change myself
> With lots of help from You.

Looking up today in your dictionary

The center of morning is
Rosy bud pink.
The afternoon fence is
Pasture sky blue.
The pendant of twilight
Shines bright as a star.
I touch me, surprised
That I am still here,
Without drink,
Under You.

Spring birth

Baby robin breaks the shell
Of private inward citadel.
Wet and helpless, weak of wing,
She reaches out toward birds that sing.
Painful, though it is to break,
Loss of shell-self heals her heart.

Three forward, two back

The mountain top
Is far above.
I start and stop.
I slowly move
With faltering steps
That hold their own,
And sometimes let
Me travel up.

I can't perfect
My stumbling tracks,
But, just like other
Human folks,
Making mistakes,
I still move on.
Imperfect, weak,
I walk my steps.

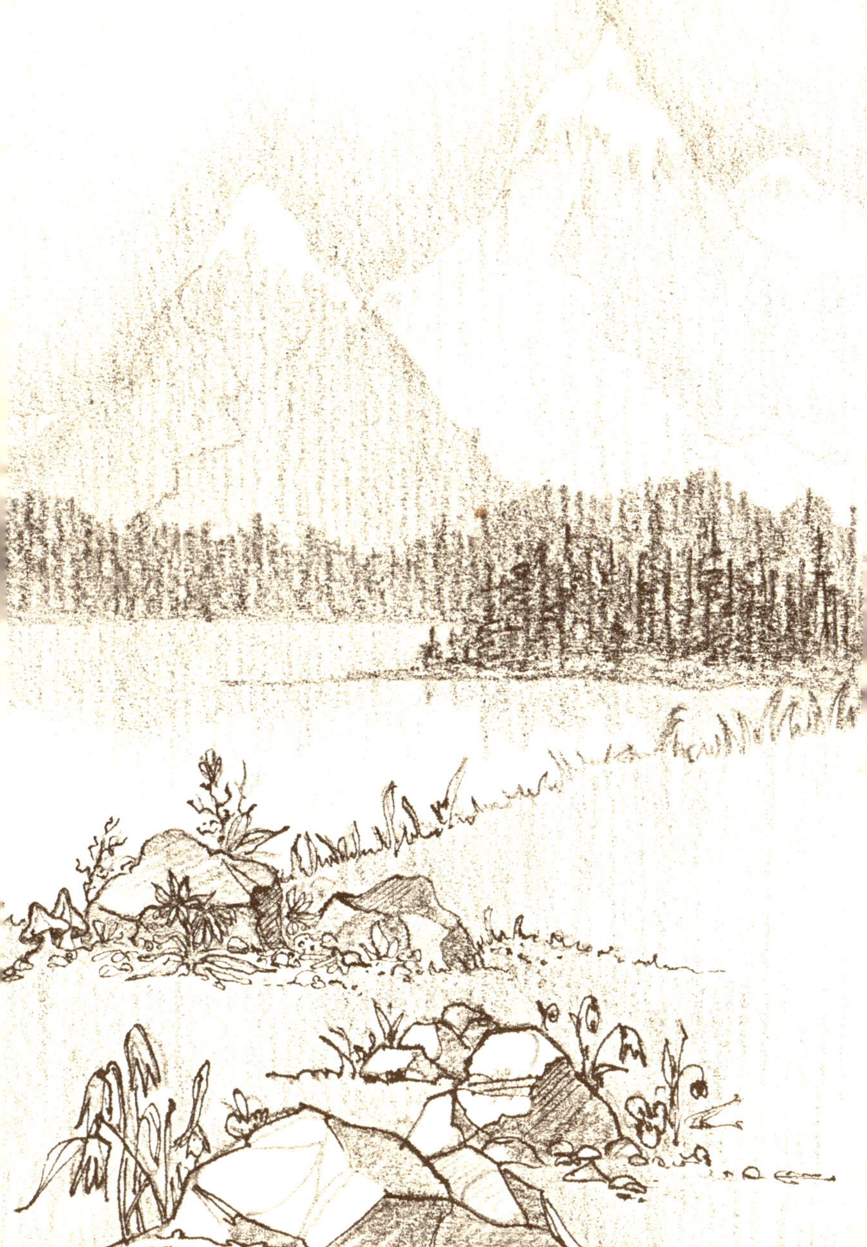

The miracle of the pussy willows

I was lost and lonely when
You came into my soul.
Then pussy willow branches
Started to grow
In a vase of hard steel.
These branches that I feel
Are silver, soft, brown, strong, and real.

Coming ashore

I feel like a beachball,
As I bounce up and down,
But I know I'll feel better
As I stick around.

The waves left behind
Crash like dungeons of sand,
And the jagged rocks, I'm finding,
Were carved by my own hand.

Spring cleaning

I walk from yesterday's telephone wires
Strung with beads of sorrow.
I pull my mind from street lights wearing
False halos of tomorrow.
I change the baby's diaper as
I look about the room,
Glad that I am capable of
Sweeping with a broom.

Admitting myself

I hammered nails through the palms of our hands,
And through our weary feet.
I closed my eyes to budding blossoms,
And would not eat
That spiritual food that heals the sick soul.
There are deaths in that drugged and drunken life I never can heal.

This sickness that makes me want a sponge filled
With a vinegar that stagnates me and my world,
I give it to You, for I know I can't save
Anyone, or anything, including myself. Wanting to live,
A miracle in itself, I turn over hammer and nails,
Self-gratification, escape, institutions, and jails.

Mother's day

The children aren't here.
Their gifts are on display:
Consequence of drinking
And drugging away
All that is precious and
All that is dear.

Fruition

I can't grow a garden,
Until I plant a seed.
I can't gather fruit,
Unless I root the weed.
I can't have my harvest
Without some days of rain,
For if I sit and dream in sun
Alone, I'm barren land.

Morning glory loom

Why the morning glory
Opens its blue face,
And reaches outward, upward,
With simple grace;
Whether roots, or leaves,
Whether vine
Is so unimportant
In surrender's design.
It is the daily trace
Of flowers to weaver, though blind,
That brings inner peace.

Mother's day bouquet

My daughters plant a lilac bush
As easily as love
That gives and does not count the cost
And slowly grows.
Together we are healing
And turning toward the spring
You offer beyond winter,
Like lilacs, blossoming.

Spiritual blackout

I was on a dry drunk
In a desert of sand.
Nothing spiritual lived
In that land.

I lashed out
Like a windmill gone mad,
With parched throat.
Finally it passed, a sad

Sunset; a grief
Of vacant twilight.
Beside me, my sister
Told me it was all right.

Without wound, she touched me,
And understood,
So glad it was dry
And finally found God.

Relativity

I have seen the annihilating
Cold white moon,
And the dark earth feeding
Her children,
Often enough to see,
When I look,
That sometimes darkness is good, and
Light is sick.

Belief is knowledge of the heart

I walked through death unnumbered times,
And yet I did not die;
I shook the dice of life beyond
Box cars and snake eyes.
My own heart beating in my chest
Is not a total fool,
For it has come to believe in
You and miracles.

Prodigal daughter

There was an example
That couldn't perfect
The life that he lived,
Nor reach for the hands outstretched.

His umbrella kept dry
The souls underneath,
And hands went to work,
As muscled feet

Set print by print
A path I could follow.
A mouth blessed me with truth
That love helped me to swallow.

I walk in those footprints
Though the walker is not here.
They still keep me sober.
That walk is my prayer.

Madame butterfly learning to d‹

There is no cure,
But to recover,
To join the butterflies
Full measure:
Wings beautiful
In our pieces of color,
Fragilely
Attached to a scar,
That must move carefully
Among the dandelions and the stars,
As from that weakness,
Our wings stretch out full length,
Reaching to help,
The scar our source
Of strength.

e Twelfth Step

Layover

The plane sets me down
In a city, unknown,
I reach out
For the telephone.

You are still there.
Direct dialing provides
Local help as I travel
The cross country road.

Separation

This is the lawyer's office.
We try to agree
On how to separate
Amicably.

I do not walk it well.
It hurts like hell.
Revenge, rage,
Lock me in a cage

Of my own destruction.
Separation?
The sky severed by lightning?
This hard wall, fighting

Reality, the agony
Of this disease I re-embrace,
Finally brings me down
On my knees, looking up into Your face.

Into reality

Into my motives I move,
Asking myself if I
Really want to keep dying
Above the tree tops, high.

There are prices in this world
For the self building walls
In front of the self. Unless
I don't mind the long fall

Into the sauce, I must strive
To pull off my own delusions
And live my real life only
Without false illusions.

The seven veils of autumn fall

The wind blows fantasies
From the trees,
Revealing
The real
Branch, naked and unafraid
Of its knots and scars.
There is no longer need
To decorate its limbs
With
Make believe
Stars.

Leaf raking

I stop to rake the leaves, today.
Tomorrow they'll be blown away . . .

I take my little girls, and I,
I rake until, in leaves piled high,
They tumble, one and one,
Underneath the Indian sun.
(. . . A little extra summer, a reprieve . . .)

With the leaves
I bury them and they bury me —
The three of us together.
Soon enough there will be colder weather.
And so, with dishes sitting on the shelf,
I take myself

Outside, to rake the leaves today . . .
Tomorrow they'll be blown away.

Salvation song for an ant

The ant picks up a crumb
Much bigger than himself.
You never see him run,
Nor strain a drop of the wealth

From that strength within.
Leverage, You, and other ants
Help him save his skin,
In his survival dance

That slowly, ever slowly, carries crumb
By crumb the necessary food for him.

Turning in the empties for you

That bottle did not love me,
Nor did those chemicals.
I open and I listen
To singing miracles.

I, powerless and empty,
Surrender totally.
I know I cannot walk alone.
You walk with me.

Peeling off my facial mask

The mask is gone,
And I stand here,
Stripped, alone,
Honest, bare.

The hollow laugh
That touched no joy
Goes with the costume
And display.

You always saw
The mask of clay,
And, yet, You loved me,
Anyway.

Momentary success

This booze, these drugs
Have been my cancer cells
That fed upon me, body
Mind and soul,

And taught my hand to obey
The sick need
Of addict. It's hard to
Love, heal, and feed

Myself back to health,
But, with Your help,
Today I succeed.

Giving thanks

I sit at the table
Surrounded by Friends.
The turkey is filled with
Love and stuffing.
We've gathered together
This Thanksgiving Day,
Sober and clean,
As all of us pray
That You will continue
To keep us this way.

Candle lighting

My soul turned into
Blackened wick,
Empty, lonely,
Inward, sick.

Then You came,
Like Life and Love,
And touched the wick,
Illuminative.

Christmas
without manger

My bars, to me,
Were aluminum trees,
Gigantic, standing in malls,
Covered with electric bulbs.
I see the gifts
Beneath their feet.
I open them,
And in them meet
The hollowness
Of scarecrows filled
With straw that long
For Mary's child.

Downtown Christmas

I know there is a manger,
For I have seen a Child
Filled with You, spilling You,
Walking in the wild.

Within the inner city shine
Lost Stars of Bethlehem.
I thank You for the blessing of
The Lion and the Lamb.

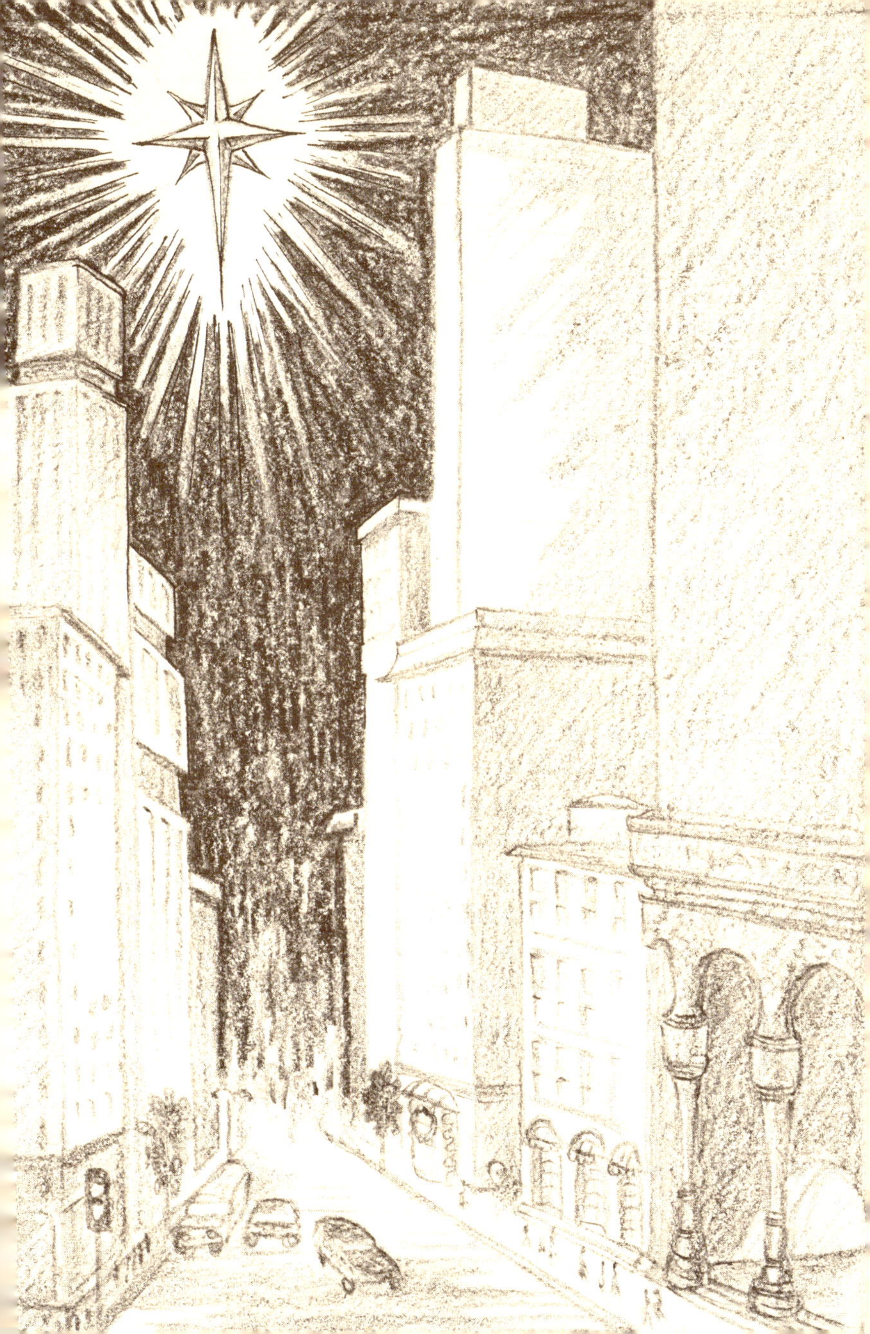

Ruination, the foundation

The lengths were not easy:
The things left behind
To salvage the body
The soul and the mind.

His words help me walk it
From somewhere above,
Though I couldn't quote him
Exactly, the love

Came through with its message:
"My other life stunk!
My worst day sober will always be
Far better than any day drunk!"

Help on the road

Sometimes it's hard
To walk my mile.
Thanks
For your smile,

Two year old blues with an upbeat

The terrible two's
Are a mother's blues.
Somehow I survive,
Intact, and alive.

And just when I'm ready
To throw in the towel,
He climbs up and kisses me,
With angelic smile.

That little girl with her curl,
Has nothing on my tot,
Professor of rages,
Innocence, and pity pots.

But when he is happy,
He's such a good friend,
Making family a blessing,
My little godsend.

The outstretched hand

Hands reach through darkness
Forming a chain,
Circling my soul.
I live once again.

I reach through that darkness.
Dawn breaks into light,
As I find those hands offer
Love from the heart.

Snow sonnet

A poinsettia flamed in the middle of snow.
Frozen there, the burning was slow
And agonizing to watch or endure.
(Either role leaves scars so deep
Returning takes a lifetime to keep
The flames from ever coming back.)
I turned, too burned, too many times,
And left the flaming flower behind.
I put out my body with my own bare hands,
Knowing that I could no longer stand
To stare and burn. Remembering
A time when it happened before, and before,
And before, and before, and before, and before . . .
I pray for myself — the blossoms innumerable.

In an emergency, halt!

Hungry, have I had three squares?
Angry, have I prayed for peace?
Lonely, have I touched a friend?
Tired, have I slept enough?

> People and You care.
> Tears bring release.
> Darkness always ends.
> This, too, shall pass.

Why me?

Why me?
Why not?
God didn't create me
To sit on a pity pot.

Ready or not, get off the pity pot

Feeling sorry, like a leaf,
Wrapped around the limb of grief,
I found that I was all alone,
In empty or in crowded room.

What good is all that pity,
Except to smother heart?
Unfolding, I touch other leaves,
For tears are impotent.

Becoming a hand

You reached into that pit
Of hallucinations,
And, for some reason, saw fit
To grant me salvation.
I am a miracle,
Brought back from death many
moons, like the rest of You.
I ask You, is it any wonder
I reach my hand
Into the drowning lake,
Trying to help You stand,
Or that I pray daily You'll escape?

Quiz for the living

Have I learned how to live?
Have I learned how to give
To the friend who is suffering still?
Have I learned how to love?
Have I learned how to move
Down the path of Your difficult will?
Have I learned how to need?
Have I done a good deed
In return for the help with my climb?
Have I learned how to pray?
Did I reach out today
To the face of You here by my arm?

80 miles of bad road

I walk up the steps
   Beyond reach of a bar,
     Never to return
       Anymore.
         It's closing time,
      But I'm okay.
     This door swings
   Both ways:
  I'm only a poem
From You.

Now that the building is gone,
  Walk with me, now.

Walking with God

God never gives me
More than my back
Can hold; nor more
Than my heart can take.

Turning to Him,
He answers each prayer:
"Yes . . .," "No . . .," or "Wait . . .,"
Then walks with me there.

Preservation

Thirst is given water,
Stranger is given home,
Along a path that leads
Directly out of storm.

The naked are all clothed,
The prisoners visited,
As children follow children
Wherever You lead.

Physical and spiritual
Recovery unexplained:
Who is healing whom is
Your miracle divine.

Snowbells

Snowbells, praying gracefully,
What made you finally bend,
And seek beyond yourself to touch
An outstretched hand?

My story is not different from
Your story or your ghosts.
Kneeling here beside you,
My soul is warm toast.

One fine day at a time

... My yesterdays will not return,
With brilliant flowers and searing burns;
I celebrate the living fern ...
                I leave the past.

... Tomorrow is not here today;
I sail away from misted spray
Of wishing waves, so far away ...
                A dreamy mast.

... This fine day, with open eyes,
I sing with birds, their happy cries
Of children, simple miracles ...
                I live at last.

Sobriety is a sunrise

Sobriety is a sunrise,
Returning from the grave.
I do not wear it like a shroud.
I sing. I dance. I live.

A gift is not a punishment.
The dues are paid, the dying done.
Radiant today, I blossom
With the rising sun.

Threefold healing

I feel
   Me heal physically,
   My body growing strong.
I feel
   Me heal mentally,
   My mind becoming sound.
I feel
   Me heal spiritually
   My soul awakening,
   As leaf, on leaf, on leaf I grow,
   A shamrock blessed with spring.

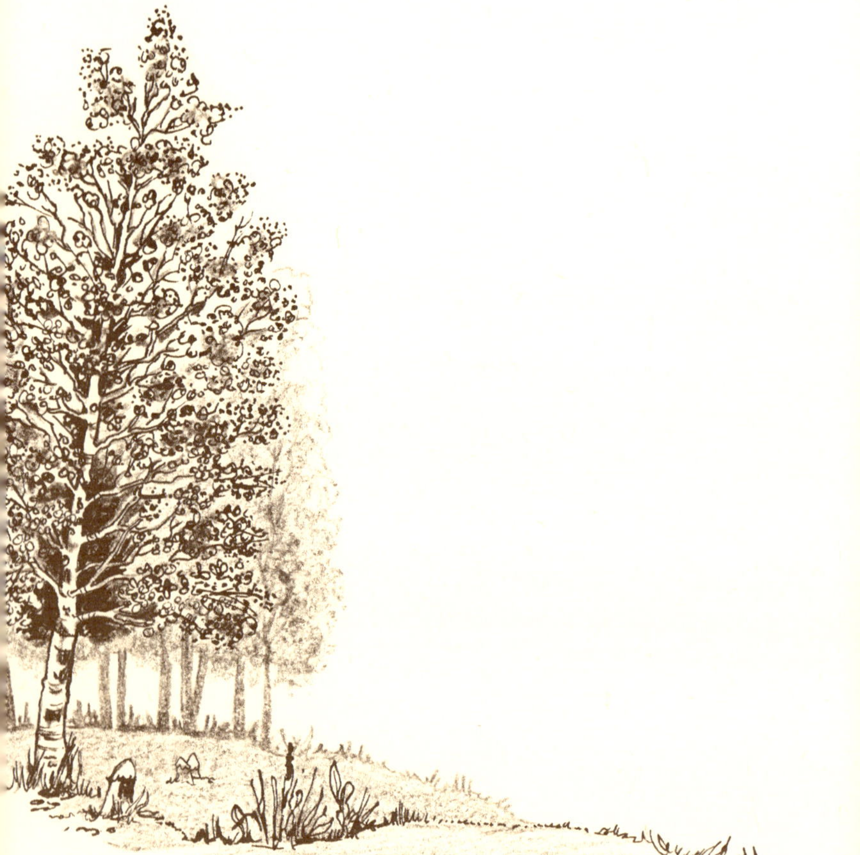